Being a
Writer™

SECOND EDITION

First edition published 2007. Second edition 2014.

Being a Writer is a trademark of Center for the Collaborative Classroom.

Center for the Collaborative Classroom wishes to thank the following authors, agents, and publishers for their permission to reprint materials included in this program. Every effort has been made to trace the ownership of copyrighted material and to make full acknowledgment of its use. If errors or omissions have occurred, they will be corrected in subsequent printings, provided that notification is submitted in writing to the publisher.

Excerpts from *In November* by Cynthia Rylant, text copyright © 2000 by Cynthia Rylant. Reprinted by permission of Houghton Mifflin Harcourt Publishing Company. All rights reserved. Excerpts from *My Father's Hands* by Joanne Ryder. Copyright © 1994 by Joanne Ryder. Used by permission of HarperCollins Publishers. "First Day of School," "How I Saved a Dog's Life," and "Believing in Myself" from *Kids Write Through It: Essays from Kids Who Have Triumphed Over Trouble*. Copyright © 1998 Fairview Press. Reprinted with permission of Fairview Press. Excerpts from *Grandma's Records* by Eric Velasquez copyright © 2001. Reprinted by permission of Walker & Co. Excerpt from *Childtimes: A Three-Generation Memoir* copyright © 1979 by Eloise Greenfield and Lessie Jones Little. Used by permission of HarperCollins Publishers. Excerpts from *Cherries and Cherry Pits* by Vera Williams. Text copyright © 1986 Vera Williams. Used by permission of HarperCollins Publishers. Excerpts from *Tacky the Penguin* by Helen Lester. Copyright © 1988 by Helen Lester. Reprinted by permission of Houghton Mifflin Harcourt Publishing Company. All rights reserved. Excerpts from *The Paper Bag Princess* text copyright © 1980 Bob Munsch Enterprises, published by Annick Press. Reproduced by permission. Excerpt from *Scarecrow* by Cynthia Rylant. Text copyright © 1998 by Cynthia Rylant. Reprinted by permission of Houghton Mifflin Harcourt Publishing Company. All rights reserved. Excerpts from *Julius, the Baby of the World* by Kevin Henkes. Copyright © 1990 by Kevin Henkes. Used by permission of HarperCollins Publishers. Excerpt from *Into the Sea* copyright © 1996 by Brenda Guiberson. Illustrations © 1996 by Alix Berenzy. Reprinted by permission of Henry Holt & Company. All rights reserved. Excerpt from *A Pack of Wolves and Other Canine Groups* by Anna Claybourne. Copyright © 2013 by Heinemann Library, an imprint of Capstone Global Library, LLC Chicago, Illinois. All rights reserved. Excerpt from *Panda Kindergarten* by Joanne Ryder. Copyright © 2009 by Joanne Ryder. Used by permission of HarperCollins Publishers. "Dolphin" from *1-2-3 Draw Ocean Life* by Freddie Levin. Copyright © 2005, published by Peel Productions, www.123draw.com. Reprinted by permission of Peel Productions. "Bottlenose Dolphin" from *Doodle a Zoodle* © 2006 by Deborah Zemke. Used by permission of Blue Apple Books. "Puzzle Sticks" from *Fun-To-Make Crafts for Every Day*. Copyright © 2005 by Boyds Mills Press. Reprinted by permission. "Galoshes" from *Stories to Begin On* by Rhoda W. Bacmeister. Copyright 1940 by E.P. Dutton, renewed © 1968 by Rhoda W. Bacmeister. Used by permission of Dutton Children's Books, a division of Penguin Group (USA) LLC. "Two Voices in a Tent at Night" from *Toasting Marshmallows: Camping Poems* by Kristine O'Connell George. Copyright © 2001 by Kristine O'Connell George. Reprinted by permission of Clarion Books, an imprint of Houghton Mifflin Harcourt Publishing Company. All rights reserved. "Fresh Pop-Corn" excerpted from *Lettuce Introduce You: Poems about Food* by Laura Purdie Salas. Copyright © 2009 by Capstone Press, an imprint of Capstone. All rights reserved. "Which is the Best?" by James Stevenson from *Poetry Speaks to Children* edited by Elise Paschen. Text copyright © 2001 by James Stevenson. Used by permission of HarperCollins Publishers. "Sunning" by James S. Tippett appears in *The Seasons*. Copyright © 2005, edited by John N. Serio. Published by Sterling Publishing Co. "The Polliwogs" from *Lizards, Frogs, and Polliwogs* by Douglas Florian. Copyright © 2001 by Douglas Florian. Reprinted by permission of Houghton Mifflin Harcourt Publishing Company. All rights reserved. "It's Raining!" from *Come To My Party and Other Shape Poems* copyright © 2004 by Heidi Roemer. Reprinted by permission of Henry Holt & Company. All rights reserved. "Ice Cubes" from *Splish Splash* by Joan Bransfield Graham. Text copyright © 1994 by Joan Bransfield Graham. Illustration copyright © 1994 by Steven Scott. Reprinted by permission of Houghton Mifflin Harcourt Publishing Company. All rights reserved. "Open Hydrant" from *Sun Through the Window* by Marci Ridlon. Copyright © 1996 by Marci Ridlon. Published by Wordsong, an imprint of Boyds Mills Press. Reprinted by permission. Illustration by Arnold Lobel from *The Random House Book of Poetry for Children* selected by Jack Prelutsky, copyright © 1983 by Random House. Used by permission of Random House Children's Books, a division of Random House LLC. All rights reserved. "Autumn Leaves" from *Jamboree: Rhymes for All Times* by Eve Merriam. Copyright © 1962, 1964, 1966, 1973, 1984 by Eve Merriam. Used by permission of Marian Reiner. "Hotel Swimming Pool's Lament" from *Barefoot: Poems for Naked Feet* by Stefi Weisburd. Copyright © 2008 by Stefi Weisburd. Published by Wordsong, an imprint of Boyds Mills Press. Reprinted by permission. "Oak's Introduction" from *Old Elm Speaks: Tree Poems* by Kristine O'Connell George. Copyright © 1998 by Kristine O'Connell George. Reprinted by permission of Clarion Books, an imprint of Houghton Mifflin Harcourt Publishing Company. All rights reserved.

All articles and texts reproduced in this manual and not referenced with a credit line above were created by Center for the Collaborative Classroom.

Cover illustration by Michael Wertz

Center for the Collaborative Classroom
1001 Marina Village Parkway, Suite 110
Alameda, CA 94501
(800) 666-7270; fax: (510) 464-3670
collaborativeclassroom.org

ISBN 978-1-61003-255-1

Printed in the United States of America

13 14 15 16 17 BNG 25 24 23 22 21 20 19 18

Being a Writer™

SECOND EDITION

Excerpts

from *In November*
by Cynthia Rylant

In November, the earth is growing quiet. It is making its bed, a winter bed for flowers and small creatures. The bed is white and silent, and much life can hide beneath its blankets.

In November, the trees are standing all sticks and bones. Without their leaves, how lovely they are, spreading their arms like dancers. They know it is time to be still.

still

In November, the smell of food is different. It is an orange smell. A squash and a pumpkin smell. It tastes like cinnamon and can fill up a house in the morning, can pull everyone from bed in a fog. Food is better in November than any other time of the year.

A squash and a pumpkin smell

In November, at winter's gate, the stars are brittle. The sun is a sometime friend. And the world has tucked her children in, with a kiss on their heads, till spring.

winter's gate

from *My Father's Hands*
by Joanne Ryder

He calls to me with a promise in his voice, and I run, seeing his hands curl like a flower budding, then unfolding wide so I can see . . . the leaf-green mantis balancing today on long thin legs. . . .

Gently my father tips his hands, softly urging the small one to my open palms. Green prickly feet find their footing on my steady fingers. The mantis tilts his pointed face, his huge round eyes watching me watch him. He is so light, so bold, so strange. I wonder what he thinks of me, of my hands soft and warm.

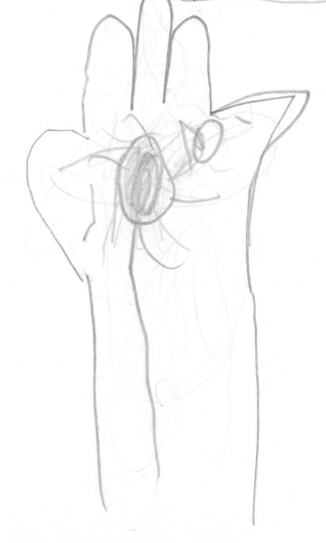

First Day of School

by Jennifer, age 10, from *Kids Write Through It: Essays from Kids Who Have Triumphed Over Trouble*

When I first started going to school, I was scared that the other kids might laugh at me. I had never been to school before, and I didn't really know what to think. I remember when I first saw my classroom I felt bad and started to cry. I instantly knew I wanted my mom, but when I looked back, my mom was gone. Being in a strange place, I wasn't sure everyone was friendly, and now that my mom was gone, I started to cry even more. My teacher came to me and kindly told me that everything was going to be fine. That didn't help right away, but after a while I felt better about being there.

Having a kind teacher and friends who were nice to me on my first day of school makes this memory a good one. If you ask me what I learned on my first day of school, I'd tell you that even though you're in a new place doing something you never did before, and it's uncomfortable, if you look for kind faces and be yourself, it'll be all right. Kind faces and loving acts can make everything around you seem a little better.

Opening Sentences from Four Personal Narratives

Every year, right after the last day of school, I'd pack a suitcase with my cool summer clothes, my favorite toys, and a sketchbook. Then my dog, Daisy, and I were off to Grandma's apartment in El Barrio.

— from *Grandma's Records*

A terrible thing happened to my brother John in the schoolyard one day.

— from "John and the Snake" (*Childtimes*)

When I first started going to school, I was scared that the other kids might laugh at me.

— from "First Day of School"

When my old dog, Winston, died, it was sad for all of us. So one day we went to the SPCA to look for a new dog. Of course, I knew we could never, ever, replace Winston, but if I didn't have a dog I would be sad forever.

— from "How I Saved a Dog's Life"

Closing Sentences from Three Personal Narratives

Even now, when I'm playing CDs in my studio, I imagine I'm back in Grandma's living room and she turns to me and says, "You be the DJ today. *Siempre me gusta tu selección.*" And as I work, Grandma's special song surrounds me.

— from *Grandma's Records*

No one will ever bring me better treasures than the ones cupped in my father's hands.

— from *My Father's Hands*

I hope my story will help other children with learning disabilities to overcome their fears and to believe in themselves. I hope each of them will become the confident person that I have become.

— from "Believing in Myself"

from *Cherries and Cherry Pits*

by Vera B. Williams

THIS is the train seat. And THIS is a tiny white woman sitting on the train seat. She is almost as short as I am, but she is a grandmother. On her head is a black hat with a pink flower, like a rose flower. It has shiny green leaves, like the leaves in my uncle's florist shop. On her feet are old, old shoes. These are the buckles. And in her lap is a big black pocketbook.

———————————————————

"You like it?" asks the lady. "You like cherries, honeybird?" She laughs and dumps all of the cherries onto the geranium plant in front of the parrot. "There's your own little cherry tree," she says to the parrot. She stands next to the geranium in her stocking feet, eating cherries with the parrot.

———————————————————

And this boy is tall like my brother. And he has glasses like my brother. And the same kind of cap. And the same green and black jacket, too. It has the orange letters from his team. And when he smiles you can see the space between his big front teeth like my brother's.

———————————————————

When he gets off the train at his station, he just runs right up the escalator. He runs right along the streets, jumping on and off the stoops to his house. Before he even gets up the stairs, and he can take them in just two steps, he's hollering to his little sister. "Hey, come on out here. See what I got for you."

Closing Sentences from Three Stories

Goodly, Lovely, Angel, Neatly, and Perfect hugged Tacky. Tacky was an odd bird but a very nice bird to have around.

— from *Tacky the Penguin*

"Ronald," said Elizabeth, "your clothes are really pretty and your hair is very neat. You look like a real prince, but you are a bum."

They didn't get married after all.

— from *The Paper Bag Princess*

The wind is brushing his borrowed head
and the sun is warming his borrowed hands
and clouds are floating across his button-borrowed eyes.
The scarecrow is thinking his long, slow thoughts . . .
. . . and soon, birds will be coming by.

— from *Scarecrow*

from *Julius, the Baby of the World*
by Kevin Henkes

After Julius was born, it was a different story.
Lilly took her things back.
She pinched his tail.
And she yelled insulting comments into his crib.

_____

But her parents loved him.
They kissed his wet pink nose.
They admired his small black eyes.
And they stroked his sweet white fur.

_____

Lilly's parents were dazzled when Julius babbled and gurgled.
"Such a vocabulary!" they exclaimed.
But if Lilly did the exact same thing, they said,
"Lilly, let's act our age, please."

_____

Lilly's nose twitched.
Her eyes narrowed.
Her fur stood on end.
And her tail quivered.

from *Tacky the Penguin*
by Helen Lester

Every day Goodly, Lovely, Angel, Neatly, and Perfect greeted each other quietly and politely.

Tacky greeted them with a hearty slap on the back and a loud "What's happening?"

_____

"PENNNNGUINS?" said Tacky. "Do you mean those birds that march neatly in a row?"

And he marched, 1-2-3, 4-2, 3-6-0, 2½, 0.

The hunters looked puzzled.

"Do you mean those birds that dive so gracefully?" Tacky asked.

And he did a splashy cannonball.

The hunters looked wet.

"Do you mean those birds that sing such pretty songs?"

Tacky began to sing, and from behind the block of ice came the voices of his companions, all singing as loudly and dreadfully as they could.

"HOW MANY TOES DOES A FISH HAVE? AND HOW MANY WINGS ON A COW?

I WONDER. YUP, I WONDER."

Speech Punctuation in Two Stories

"What's happening?" blared Tacky, giving one hunter an especially hearty slap on the back.

They growled, "We're hunting for penguins. That's what's happening."

— from *Tacky the Penguin*

Elizabeth said, "Dragon, is it true that you can fly around the world in just ten seconds?"

"Why, yes," said the dragon and jumped up and flew all the way around the world in just ten seconds.

He was very tired when he got back, but Elizabeth shouted, "Fantastic, do it again!"

— from *The Paper Bag Princess*

Interesting Introductions from Three Nonfiction Books

Tap, tap. Scritch. The tiny sea turtle is the last hatchling to break out of her leathery egg and crawl up the sides of a sandy nest. She is not much bigger than a bottle cap and would make a good meal for a hungry sea bird or a crab.

— from *Into the Sea*

When you think of a wolf, you might think of wolves in movies, cartoons, and fairy tales. Some are shown as wild, bloodthirsty beasts, howling at the Moon. They also appear as werewolves (half wolf and half human creatures) in horror stories, or as the big, bad villain who eats Red Riding Hood's grandmother . . . So, what are real wolves like? You might be surprised.

— from *A Pack of Wolves and Other Canine Groups*

One panda cub is a sight to see. Two panda cubs together is rare. But imagine seeing sixteen young giant pandas all at once! Meet a panda kindergarten class at the Wolong Nature Reserve in China, where pandas are protected, loved, and given great care.

— from *Panda Kindergarten*

Closing Sentences from Three Informational Reports

Chameleons are pretty unusual animals. Some people may think they are weird, but I think they are awesome. Their changing skin color, swiveling eyes, and long, sticky tongues make them different from most animals. I hope that you have enjoyed reading about chameleons. The next time you go to the zoo, you should definitely visit these amazing lizards.

— by Tamar

As you have learned, mountain gorillas are endangered animals. Humans have destroyed much of their habitat and sometimes even hunted them. However, there is still hope for the gorillas. Scientists and nature lovers around the world are working to protect mountain gorillas and save their habitat. These gentle, intelligent, and magnificent animals are special, and I would be very sad if they became extinct.

— by Caleb

Spiders may be small, but they can do things that make people say "Wow!" They can spin very strong webs. Some spiders have poison that is powerful enough to kill animals or even people. They can live in almost any habitat on Earth. As you now know, spiders have been around for a long time—they first appeared 300 million years ago—and I think they will be here for millions more.

— by Ana

Dolphin

from *1-2-3 Draw Ocean Life* by Freddie Levin

Dolphin

(6 to 13 feet long)

A dolphin is not a fish. It is a mammal that lives in the ocean. Mammals give birth and nurse their babies. A dolphin uses its tail to swim. Playful, friendly dolphins come to the surface and breathe air through their blow holes. They communicate in a language of clicks and squeaks.

1 Look at the shapes and lines in the first drawing. Lightly sketch a small circle for the head. Draw a small eye. Start the dolphin's body with two curved lines.

2 Draw the dolphin's snout. It's called a 'beak.' Add a dorsal fin.

3 Draw two flippers. Using curved lines, add the tail.

4 Look at the final drawing. Erase extra sketch lines. Shade and color your dolphin.

Bottlenose Dolphin

from *Doodle a Zoodle* by Deborah Zemke

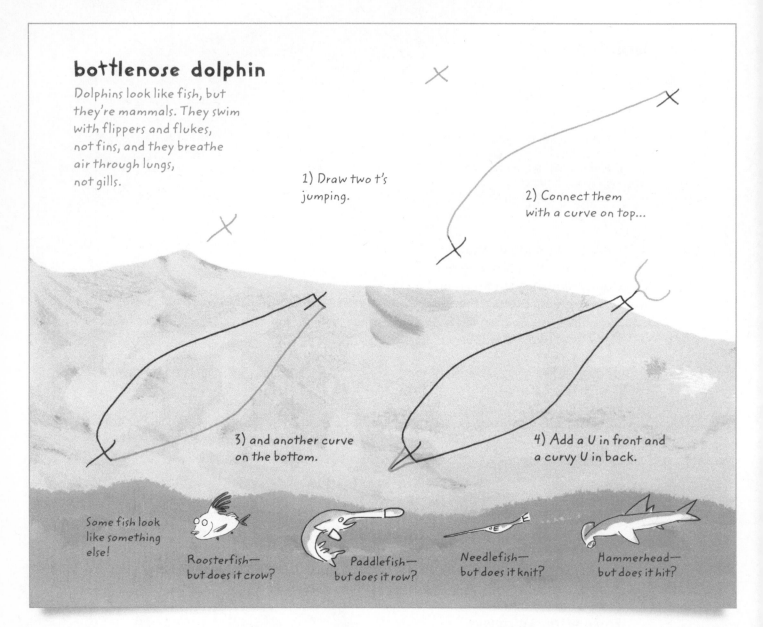

bottlenose dolphin

Dolphins look like fish, but they're mammals. They swim with flippers and flukes, not fins, and they breathe air through lungs, not gills.

1) Draw two t's jumping.

2) Connect them with a curve on top...

3) and another curve on the bottom.

4) Add a U in front and a curvy U in back.

Some fish look like something else!

Roosterfish— but does it crow?

Paddlefish— but does it row?

Needlefish— but does it knit?

Hammerhead— but does it hit?

(continues)

Bottlenose Dolphin *(continued)*

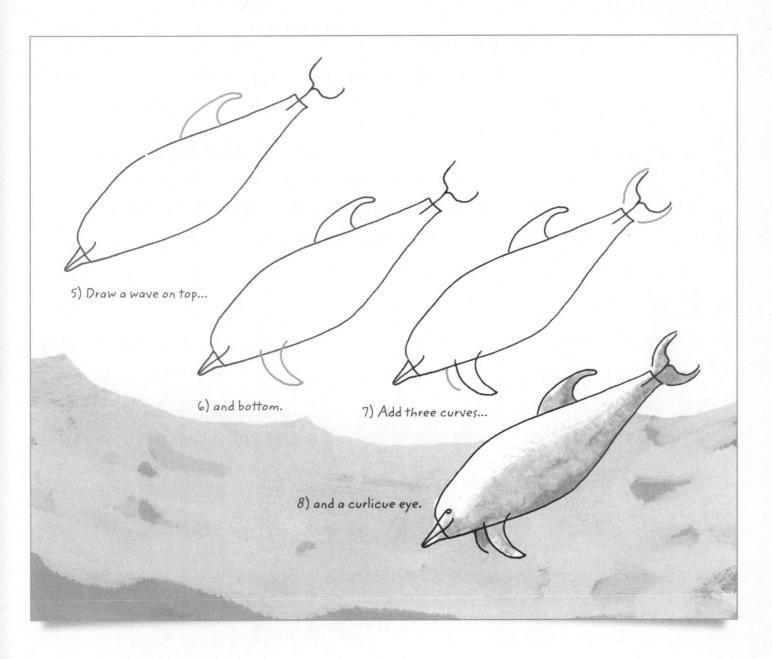

5) Draw a wave on top...

6) and bottom.

7) Add three curves...

8) and a curlicue eye.

"Bottlenose Dolphin" from *Doodle a Zoodle* © 2006 by Deborah Zemke. Used by permission of Blue Apple Books.

Puzzle Sticks

from *Fun-To-Make Crafts for Every Day,*
edited by Tom Daning

Materials: craft sticks

1. Lay twelve craft sticks side by side. Line the ends up evenly. Tape the sticks to keep them lined up, then number them from one to twelve. Flip the sticks over.

2. Use a pencil to sketch a picture on the untaped side. Color the picture with markers. Remove the tape from the back.

3. Mix up the sticks, then try to put them back together. You can make a more difficult puzzle by using more sticks.

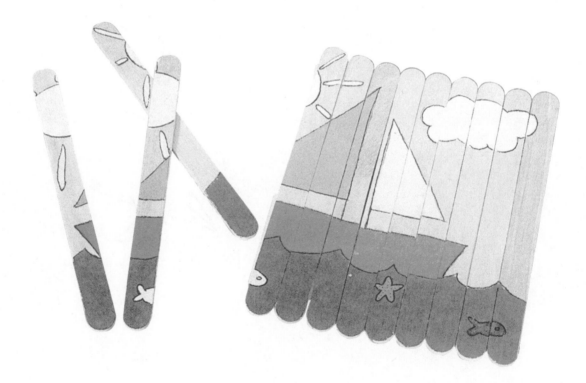

"Puzzle Sticks" from *Fun-To-Make Crafts for Every Day*. Copyright © 2005 by Boyds Mills Press. Reprinted by permission.

School Should Start Later in the Morning

I hate getting up early in the morning. It's so hard to get out of my nice warm bed. I want to sleep more! In fact, everyone should get more sleep. That's why I think school should start later in the morning.

If school started later, kids could sleep later. Then we wouldn't be so tired in class. When kids are tired, it's hard to learn. Nothing seems interesting. We just sit there yawning. We want to close our eyes and go "Zzzz . . . ." But when we get to sleep longer, we feel wide awake. We want to exercise our brains and learn new things. We should sleep longer because then we would be more awake in class and learn more. That would make teachers smile, because teachers always want kids to learn more.

Also, sleep is really good for you. Kids need a lot of sleep because it helps us grow. For example, I grew 2 inches last year. This year I want to grow 3 inches. Grown-ups need sleep, too. My mom says that she gets sick if she doesn't sleep enough. So, if school started later, everyone would sleep more in the morning. Then everyone would be healthier.

More sleep is good for everyone. Sleep helps kids learn, and that makes teachers happy. Also, sleep makes us all healthier. That's why I think school should start later in the morning. Let's all get more sleep!

Don't Change Our Start Time

Some people say that school should start later in the morning. I don't agree. There are many reasons why it's better for school to start early, at the normal time.

It would cause problems for families if school started later in the morning. Many parents take their kids to school and then go to work. They have to be at work at a certain time. They can't be late! If school started later, then those parents would have to rush to work. They might drive too fast, and that would not be safe. Also, they might arrive at work late and get into trouble.

If school started later, then it would finish later, too. That would be bad because then kids wouldn't be able to do after-school activities. Lots of kids play sports, volunteer, and do other fun things after school. For example, I play soccer every Tuesday and Thursday afternoon right after school. It's one of my favorite things to do. But if school finished later every day, I wouldn't have time for soccer.

As you can see, it wouldn't work to have school start later in the morning. It would be bad for parents, and it would be bad for kids, too. Anyway, if you really want to sleep in, that's what the weekend is for.

Rats Are the Coolest Pets

Some kids like dogs, and some kids like cats. Believe it or not, I think rats are the coolest pets. I should know because I have an amazing pet rat named Zippy. So if you're thinking of getting a pet, how about a rat? Rats are great in so many ways.

First, rats are friendly and really smart. You can teach them fun things. I taught Zippy to sit on my arm and ride around with me. I also taught him to come to me when I call his name! How smart is that? Rats are also very clean. Maybe you thought they were smelly, like some other pets. Well, I'm here to tell you that rats smell fine. Also, rats are interesting to look at. They have twinkly eyes and soft fur. If you had a pet rat, I bet everyone in your family would enjoy it.

Next, pet rats are easy to take care of. For example, they don't need to go on walks. Since rats are small, they don't even need a yard. My rat Zippy has a nice big cage, and that's his home. Also, pet rats won't mess up your stuff like dogs sometimes do. They won't chew on tables or chairs. Your parents would love that.

Now you know why I think rats are the coolest pets. They are friendly, smart, clean, and easy to take care of. If you want a pet, I think you should definitely get a rat. You will love it and so will your family!

Why You Should Get a Dog

When I walk down the street with my frisky, fluffy, brown dog, Boomer, everyone smiles at us. People just love dogs . . . they can't help it! I believe that dogs are the best pets ever.

Dogs are the best because they are loyal. That means dogs love the people who take care of them. Dogs want to make them happy. In fact, they will even protect them. For example, I read about a brave dog that saved its owner from a terrible fire. Another dog saved a boy from drowning. A cat or a rat or a bird couldn't do those things.

Also, dogs are wonderful because they come in many different shapes and sizes. Since there are so many, there is definitely a right dog for you. Maybe you want a small, cuddly dog. You can find one easily. Maybe you want a big, strong dog that loves to run and play. There are plenty of dogs like that. Maybe you have allergies, and you want a dog that won't make you sneeze. There are even dogs like that!

Last of all, having a dog is great for your health. That's because dogs need to go on walks every day. Walking is good for people, too. Did you know that most people don't get enough exercise? Walking your dog is a fun, easy way to get more exercise. You can't walk a cat or another type of pet!

If you want a pet, I really think you should get a dog. They are the most loyal, loving, and wonderful pets in the world.

Computers in Our Classrooms

We live in an amazing time. Computers are changing how we live and work. I think it is very important for schools to have enough computers for students to use.

Students need computers so we can get on the Internet. The Internet is very good for learning. There are many great websites for students. We can see videos of animals we're studying in science class. We can read interviews with famous authors. We can chat online with students in other parts of the country.

When the kids of today are all grown up, we will be living in a world filled with technology. If we don't learn how to use computers and technology now, we won't be able to get good jobs. Right now in our classroom, we have just one computer. Only one or two students at a time can use it. That means we never get enough practice with the computer. We really need more computers!

I hope that our school principal and teachers will read this. They want us to learn a lot. They want us to do great things when we grow up. That's why I think that they should try hard to get more computers for our classrooms.

Persuasive Essay Excerpts with Sentence Fragments

I think people should always pick up their trash. Trash makes our streets dirty. And sidewalks, too. When trash is everywhere, it isn't fun to walk around. Also, when people don't pick up their trash, it is bad. For nature. Plants can't grow when the ground is covered with trash. Trash can hurt animals, too. For example. An animal might eat trash and get sick.

If people picked up their own trash, it wouldn't be a problem in our city. When you see trash on the ground. Pick it up! It is easy to do. It only takes a second. Also, if you want to make a difference. Organize a clean-up day in your neighborhood. You can ask family and friends to help. When lots of people work together, cleaning up trash is not too hard. In fact, it can be fun! And a good way to make new friends.

Poem

Galoshes

by Rhoda Bacmeister

Susie's galoshes
Make splishes and sploshes
And slooshes and sloshes
As Susie steps slowly
Along in the slush.

They stamp and they tramp
On the ice and concrete,
They get stuck in the muck and the mud;
But Susie likes much best to hear

The slippery slush
As it slooshes and sloshes,
And splishes and sploshes,
All around her galoshes!

Two Voices in a Tent at Night
by Kristine O'Connell George

Shhhhh . . .
Something is scratching
on our tent.

                    Is not.

Is too.

                    Is not.

Scratching!

                    I don't hear anything.

Something is scratching!

                    Go to sleep.

It's you! Stop it!

                    No, it's *not*. It's a branch.

"It is you!"
Isn't it?

                    OK. OK. It *was* me . . .
                    Wait.
                    Something's scratching!
                    Listen.

Told you so.
Scratching!

                    Shhhhh. Are *you* doing that?

No. No. No!

                    Think it's the dog?

I hope so.

Fresh Pop-Corn
by Laura Purdie Salas

each
kernel

POPS

with a
bubblewrap
burst

sweet
buttery
corn-juice

slides
down

my
throat

Which is the Best?

by James Stevenson

Ice cream on a stick,
Covered with cold, shiny chocolate,

Or ice cream heaped up in a cone,
Dripping fast on a hot day,

Or ice cream in a big blue bowl
And a spoon you can take your time with—

Which is the best?

It is too soon
To give the answer.

I have more testing
To do.

Sunning
by James S. Tippett

Old Dog lay in the summer sun
Much too lazy to rise and run.
He flapped an ear
At a buzzing fly.
He winked a half opened
Sleepy eye.
He scratched himself
On an itching spot,
As he dozed on the porch
Where the sun was hot.
He whimpered a bit
From force of habit
While he lazily dreamed
Of chasing a rabbit.
But Old Dog happily lay in the sun
Much too lazy to rise and run.

"Sunning" by James S. Tippett appears in *The Seasons*. Copyright © 2005, edited by John N. Serio. Published by Sterling Publishing Co.

The Polliwogs
by Douglas Florian

We polliwoggle.
We polliwiggle.
We shake in lakes,
Make wakes,
And wriggle.
We quiver,
We shiver,
We jiggle,
We jog.
We're yearning
To turn ourselves
Into a frog.

It's Raining!
by Heidi B. Roemer

Pitter patter
Plip plop!
Rain falls from the Sky . . .
I open my umbrella up
and I stay dry

Ice Cubes
by Joan Bransfield Graham

ice cubes
clicking
clatter
clink

crazily
inside
my drink

crystal
chorus
clear and
bold

chattering
about
the cold

Open Hydrant
by Marci Ridlon

Water rushes up
and gushes,
cooling summer's sizzle.

In a sudden whoosh
it rushes,
not a little drizzle.

First a hush and down
it crashes,
over curbs it swishes.

Just a luscious waterfall
for
cooling city fishes.

Autumn Leaves
by Eve Merriam

Down
      down
            down
Red
      yellow
            brown
Autumn leaves tumble down,
Autumn leaves crumble down,
Autumn leaves bumble down,
Flaking and shaking,
Tumbledown leaves.

Skittery
Flittery
Rustle by
Hustle by
Crackle and crunch
In a snappety bunch.

Run and catch
Run and catch
Butterfly leaves
Sailboat leaves
Windstorm leaves.
Can you catch them?

Swoop,
Scoop,
Pile them up
In a stompy pile and
Jump
      Jump
    JUMP!

Hotel Swimming Pool's Evening Lament
by Stefi Weisburd

I've been
so bored
staring
at the sky
all day
while you
were at
the beach
playing
with the ocean.
No one to swirl me.
No one to splash, to dive.
No one to swim through me sleek
and slow. Come on, child. At least dip in a   toe.

Oak's Introduction
by Kristine O'Connell George

I've been wondering
when you'd notice
me standing here.

I've been waiting,
watching you
grow taller.

I have grown too.
My branches
are strong.

Step closer.
Let's see
how high

you can

climb.

Word Bank

able	ago	and	arguing
about	air	angry	argument
above	alive	animal	arms
absolutely	all right	another	around
accidentally	almost	answer	as
ache	along	answered	ask
across	already	any	asked
act	also	anyone	at
add	although	apart	ate
address	always	apology	athlete
advice	am	approximately	aunt
after	America	April	author
again	American	arctic	away
against	among	area	awful
age	an	argue	

baby
back
bad
bag
ball
band
base
baseball
basketball
be
beautiful
became
because
become
bed
been
beep

beetle
before
began
begin
beginning
behind
being
below
belt
beneath
best
better
between
beyond
bicycle
big
biggest

bike
bird
birds
black
blue
boat
body
book
both
bottle
bought
box
boy
bread
breakfast
breath
breathe

brick
bridge
bring
broke
brought
building
built
bunny
buried
bury
bus
busy
butter
button
buy

B

C

cabin	cent	clear	courageous
came	certain	close	course
camp	chair	cloth	cover
candy	change	coal	covered
cannot	charge	coat	crack
captain	check	cold	crackle
car	cheer	color	crayon
carefully	cheese	come	creak
carrot	cherry	coming	creep
carry	chief	common	crib
carrying	children	complete	cricket
cartoon	chocolate	conquer	cried
cast	choose	consider	crowd
cat	circle	contain	cry
ceiling	circus	control	cupboard
celebrate	city	correct	cut
cemetery	class	couldn't	

C

D

dairy	desk	discover	dream
danger	develop	disease	dribble
dangerous	die	dive	drink
dark	difference	do	drop
dear	different	doctor	dropped
decided	dime	does	drove
decision	dining	dog	drowned
decorate	dinner	don't	dry
deep	dinosaur	done	during
defense	dirty	door	dust
definitely	disappear	double	
describe	disappoint	draw	

D

E

each
early
earth
easily
east
easy
eat
eggs

elbow
embarrass
empty
end
English
enough
environment
equation

equipment
even
ever
every
everybody
everywhere
example
excellent

except
excitement
exercise
exhausted
explain
extremely
eye

E

F

face	feet	fish	fourth
facet	felt	five	free
fact	fence	fix	Friday
fall	few	flew	friend
family	field	flies	friends
far	fierce	fly	front
farm	figure	follow	frown
farther	fill	food	frozen
fascinate	filled	football	fuel
fast	final	force	full
father	finally	form	funny
favorite	fine	forth	further
feather	finger	forty	future
February	finish	forward	
feed	fire	found	
feel	first	four	

F

G

game	glow	grader	grown
gave	glue	gray	guard
getting	goal	great	guess
girl	goes	green	guessed
give	good	ground	guide
glad	got	group	guilty
gloves	government	grow	gun

G

H

hair
half
halt
hand
handkerchief
happen
happened
hard
haven't
he's
head

hear
heard
heat
heavy
height
hello
help
here
heroes
high
hill

himself
hockey
hold
home
homework
hood
hoof
hook
hoop
hoping
horn

horse
hospital
hot
hour
hours
house
however
hundred
hungry
hurt

I

I'd	imaginary	include	intercept
I'll	imagine	indeed	island
I'm	important	Indian	it's
I've	impossible	innocent	its
ice	inch	inside	
idea	inches	instead	

job

join

juice

jumble

jump

junk

just

keep

kids

kind

king

kitchen

knew

knife

know

knowledge

known

J, K

L

ladder	leaf	library	looking
ladybug	learn	life	lose
lamb	leave	light	losing
land	led	lightning	lots
language	left	line	love
large	leg	liquid	loving
last	less	list	low
late	lessons	listen	lower
later	let	little	lunch
latter	letter	live	

L

M

machine	maybe	mild	mountain
mad	me	mile	mouse
magnificent	mean	milk	move
making	meant	million	Mr.
man	measure	minute	Mrs.
many	medicine	minutes	Ms.
map	melt	miss	much
mark	member	money	muscle
market	men	month	music
mass	mental	morning	must
master	met	most	myself
material	might	mother	mysterious

M

N

nail	neck	nice	note
name	need	night	nothing
napkin	nest	nine	notice
narrow	never	noise	noun
nasty	new	none	numeral
near	next	north	

N

o'clock	often	only	outside
object	oh	open	over
ocean	oil	order	own
of	old	original	
off	once	our	

P

page	people	played	protect
paid	pepper	playing	proud
pair	person	please	public
paper	pick	point	pull
parents	picture	poison	pulled
party	piece	police	punt
pass	pitch	popular	puppet
passed	place	population	purple
path	plain	power	purpose
pattern	plan	pressure	purse
paw	plane	principal	push
peace	planet	probably	put
peach	plant	problem	puzzle
penny	play	produce	

P

quarter	rain	red	rock
question	raise	regular	rocket
quick	ran	remember	rode
quickly	range	responsibility	roof
quit	rate	responsible	room
quite	reach	rest	rooster
	reached	restaurant	rough
	read	rhythm	round
	real	ride	route
	really	riding	rubber
	reason	right	rule
	receive	river	rules
	received	road	run
	recommend	roam	running

Q, R

S

sad	ship	snore	steam
safety	shoes	snow	step
said	shook	soccer	still
salt	shoot	soft	stood
same	shore	sold	stop
sandwich	short	soldier	stopped
sat	shot	solid	store
Saturday	should	some	storm
saw	show	something	story
say	shown	sometime	street
says	shriek	sometimes	strength
scared	sick	son	strong
schedule	side	song	study
school	silver	soon	studying
schoolhouse	similar	sound	stuff
science	since	south	success
scientist	sing	space	such
scientists	sit	special	sugar
sea	six	speech	summer
season	size	spell	sun
second	skateboard	spend	Sunday
seem	skis	spent	sunny
seen	sky	spoke	super
sentence	slide	sports	suppose
separate	slippery	spread	sure
serious	slowly	sprint	surely
set	small	stand	surface
seventh	snail	star	surprise
several	snare	stars	surrounded
shape	snatch	start	swallow
share	sneak	started	swamp
sheep	sneeze	state	swarm
sheet	sniffle	states	symbol
shining	snooze	stay	system

S

table	there	tired	tree
tackle	they	today	tried
take	thief	together	tries
talk	thing	told	trouble
tall	think	tomorrow	true
teacher	those	tonight	truly
tear	though	too	truth
teeth	thought	took	try
television	thousand	tool	Tuesday
tell	thousands	tooth	turn
temperature	three	top	turned
ten	through	toward	twelve
terrible	throughout	town	twenty
test	throw	toys	twice
that's	thus	train	two
their	times	travel	

U, V

under	upon	vacation
understand	us	variety
unit	used	vegetable
united	using	verb
United States	usual	victim
unless	usually	voice
until		vowel

U, V

W

wagon	weather	when	woman
wait	week	where	women
walk	weigh	which	won
walking	weird	while	wood
want	well	white	work
wanted	went	whole	world
war	were	why	worth
warm	west	wind	would
watch	wet	within	write
waves	wheel	without	writing
we're	wheels	woke	wrote

W

X, Y, Z

year	yet	you're
years	you	young
yes	you'll	your

X,Y,Z

Proofreading Notes

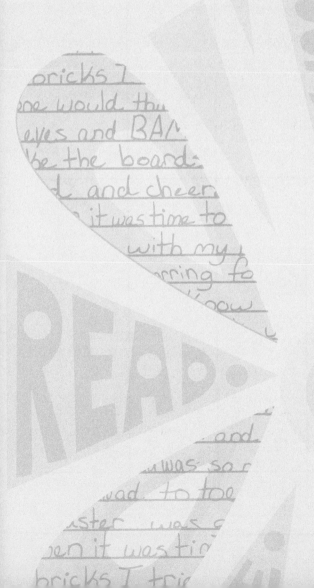
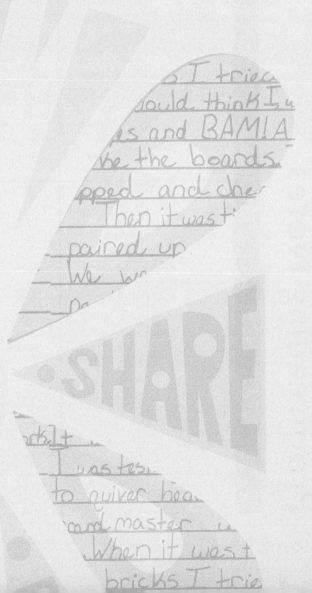

Proofreading Notes

✓	Rule	Example	Notes
☐			
☐			
☐			
☐			
☐			
☐			
☐			

Proofreading Notes

✓	Rule	Example	Notes
☐			
☐			
☐			
☐			
☐			
☐			
☐			

Proofreading Notes

✓	Rule	Example	Notes
☐			
☐			
☐			
☐			
☐			
☐			
☐			

Proofreading Notes

✓	Rule	Example	Notes
☐			
☐			
☐			
☐			
☐			
☐			
☐			

Proofreading Notes

✓	Rule	Example	Notes
☐			
☐			
☐			
☐			
☐			
☐			
☐			